carpet beetle

P9-BZJ-549

MICROSCOPIC LIFE

Theresa Greenaway

A Golden Photo Guide from St. Martin's Press

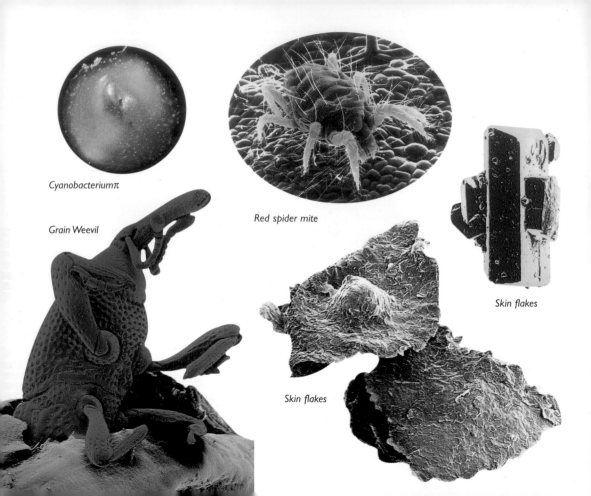

Cyanobacteriumπ

Red spider mite

Grain Weevil

Skin flakes

Skin flakes

MICROSCOPIC LIFE

A Golden Photo Guide from St. Martin's Press

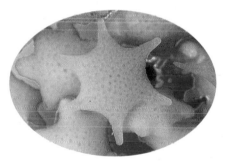

Star sand

St. Martin's Press
New York
Manufactured in China

Produced by
Elm Grove Books Limited

Series Editor Susie Elwes
Text Editor Colville Wemyss
Angela Wilkes
Art Director Lou Morley
Index Hilary Bird

Original Edition © 1998
Image Quest Limited
This edition © 2002
Elm Grove Books Limited
Text and Photographs in this book
previously published in
Eyewitness 3D Microlife

**St. Martin's Press
175 Fifth Avenue
New York, N.Y. 10010
www.stmartins.com**

A CIP catalogue record for this book is
available from the Library of Congress

ISBN 0-312-30055-7

Acknowledgments
Picture credits
Frank Greenaway 29, 45, 46; Science Photo Library 1, 1, 1, 1, 3,
3, 4, 4, 5, 5, 6, 6, 7, 8,8, 8, 9, 11, 11, 12, 14, 15, 15, 17, 17, 18, 18,
19, 19, 20, 21, 21, 21, 22, 23, 23, 25, 26, 26, 28, 31, 34, 34, 34, 35,
35, 36, 36, 38, 38, 39, 40, 44, 45, 52, 52, 54, 55, 56, 57, 58, 59;
Kim Taylor 16, 28, 30, 30, 36, 37, 44, 46, 49, 49, 52

Project Photographers
Tim Hellier, Justin Peach,
Christopher Parks, Peter Parks

The publishers would also like to thank
Brenda Green, Chris Godfrey, Leena Henman,
Bob Miller, Caroline and Victoria Moat, Abi Peach,
Julie and John Pearce

CONTENTS

SEED CAPSULE

This Scarlet Pimpernel seed capsule is only 0.2 in (5 mm) across. Examining it with a hand lens makes it look ten times bigger than it really is, and reveals how the capsule disperses its seeds.

The seeds spill out when the capsule splits across its middle.

UNDER THE MICROSCOPE

Our eyes are amazing. We can focus on detail, judge distances, and see colors in daylight. But even someone with perfect eyesight cannot see objects less than 0.0003 in (0.1 mm) across – that is, about the width of a pinpoint. To see smaller objects, and to examine closely the fine detail of larger items, we have to view them through a hand lens or a microscope. The most powerful microscopes can magnify objects a staggering 1,000–2,000 times!

BACTERIA

The minute bacteria that cause Legionnaire's disease have to be magnified 2,000 times before they can be seen clearly. They were discovered in 1976.

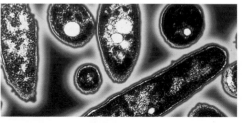

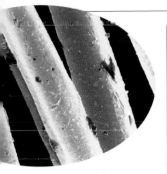

DIRTY HAIR
The outer surface of a human hair is covered with overlapping scales. When the hair becomes greasy, particles of dirt and dust cling to it.

RAINDROPS FALLING
The action of a raindrop is recorded by high-speed photography. A raindrop bounces on the surface of a puddle and pulls up a peak of water as it rises again in a column - at the top a droplet breaks off.

RED SPIDER MITE
Individual mites are difficult to see, but when they gather in huge numbers they can strip all the leaves from a plant.

As it feeds, each mite spins threads of silk to hold it tightly to the leaf.

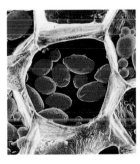

STARCH GRAINS
Inside each cell of a potato, sugary food is stored through the winter as grains of insoluble starch.
In spring, the starch is turned back into soluble sugar and carried to the growing shoots.

POTATO STARCH

Like all plants, the potato makes its own food. It stores this food as starch grains in underground roots called tubers. During cooking, the starch grains burst and make the hard potato tubers soft, floury, and tasty.

Starch grains

FOCUS ON FOOD

Put a tasty meal under our noses and the chances are we'll gobble it up without giving it a second thought. But taking a closer look at the food we eat under a microscope reveals the fascinating shapes of sugar and salt crystals, tiny grains of vegetable starch hidden in potatoes, and much more. Some food must be softened by cooking before our teeth can begin to slice, grind, and chew it into a digestible paste.

CANE SUGAR

The sweet, sticky sap pressed from sugarcane yields black molasses, golden syrup, and brown sugar. All of these contain some impurities, which can be removed by refining to leave pure white sugar crystals.

THE SAVORY SEA

Crystals of sea salt are shaped like four-sided, square-topped, hollow pyramids. They consist of sodium chloride and traces of other chemicals found in sea water.

Sea salt crystals are made by evaporating sea water from shallow pans.

SWEET CRYSTALS

Almost half of all the sugar used today is produced from the sugar beet plant. The plant's roots are crushed to produce sap, which is purified and crystallized. Beet sugar crystals are the same as the crystals refined from cane sugar.

Beet sugar crystals

Crystals of table salt are cube-shaped.

TABLE SALT

Table salt is mined from salt deposits in the ground. It is dissolved in water, washed, and crystallized into tiny cubes of pure salt (sodium chloride). Other substances are added to keep the salt dry and easy to pour.

BUDDING YEAST CELL

When a yeast cell is large enough, it multiplies by budding off a new cell. The large cell is called the mother cell, and the new bud is the known as the daughter cell.

GOOD MOLDS

For thousand of years, people have known how to make wines from grapes, beer from grains, yogurts and cheeses from milk, and bread from flour. In the 19th century it was discovered that microorganisms – such as fungi (molds and yeasts) and bacteria – are vital to each of these processes. In the 1930s, scientists made an important discovery: how to make life-saving medicines called antibiotics from microorganisms.

YEAST COLONY

In sugary or starchy liquids, yeast cells multiply so fast that short chains of cells grow before the mother and daughter cells can separate. A colony of chains and individual cells rapidly forms.

Chain of yeast cells

YEAST FROTH

Yeast feeds on sugar and produces alcohol and carbon dioxide gas. Yeast makes bread rise because bubbles of carbon dioxide trapped in the dough expand when it is heated in the oven.

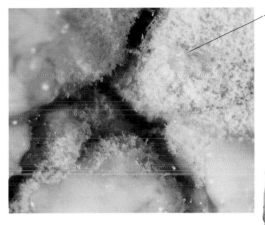

Microscopic view of cheese

TRUE BLUE VEINS

Blue spores of penicillin fungus are often injected into the cheese for extra flavor. Tiny threads spread the fungus through the cheese in a network of blue veins or streaks.

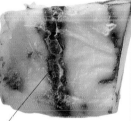

The fungus looks like blue streaks in the cheese.

Chains of this bacteria are normally found in the soil. They yield the antibiotic streptomycin, which is used to treat tuberculosis.

SOIL BACTERIA

Some bacteria naturally produce complex chemicals called antibiotics, which doctors can use to treat many diseases. Antibiotics can be manufactured for medicines by growing the bacteria in special vats that have a constant supply of air.

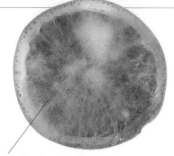

Each colored patch on this orange is a different kind of fungus. Blue-green penicillin fungi are often found on old food.

BAD MOLDS

If left uneaten, all food will eventually rot. The complex chemicals from which food is made gradually break down into simpler substances. Fungi and bacteria speed up food decay in the kitchen, just as they do in the wild. While fungus growing on food is clearly visible as mold, bacteria can only be seen with a microscope. This makes it impossible to tell with the naked eye whether or not the food has become harmful to eat.

MOLDY ORANGE
Cut in half and left uneaten, an orange develops a dense growth of fungi within a few days. The moist, sugary flesh of the orange is an ideal diet for a variety of different kinds of molds.

Masses of powdery penicillin spores are produced at the tips of tiny branches clustered on microscopic mold hairs.

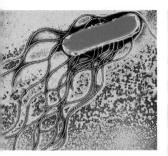

SALMONELLA
Salmonella bacteria are transmitted to food either by flies or poor standards of food processing and personal hygiene. If swallowed, salmonella can cause serious food poisoning.

This grape skin is covered with wild yeast.

MOLDY BREAD
Airborne mold spores settle on bread. As they grow, they form a covering of cottony threads on the surface of the bread, which are visible in this microscopic view.

These black-headed stalks give this fungus the name "pin-mold."

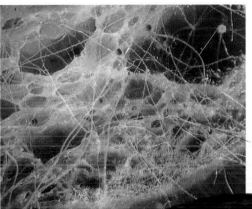

ASPERGILLUS FLAVUS
This fungus grows on stored nuts and grains, especially in damp conditions. It forms colored patches containing poisons called aflatoxins, which are very dangerous if eaten. Aflatoxins can cause liver damage and lead to cancer.

EVIL WEEVIL

The female grain weevil bores a hole into a grain of cereal and lays a single egg. She seals the hole and moves on to lay eggs in other grains. The larvae feed, grow, and pupate into adults inside the grains.

Weevil emerging from a wheat grain.

GREEDY GRUBS

The food we eat is also popular with many other animals. Some of these creatures live in our homes and share the food in our kitchens and cupboards. Insects will readily feed and breed on food left out in the open. They can also infest stored food such as grains, flour, cereals, and beans. These pests breed quickly, devouring much of the food and spoiling the remainder with their droppings, shed skin, and dead bodies.

MEALWORMS IN CEREAL

A few mealworms can ruin a whole box of cereals. The larvae of mealworm beetles are tiny when they first hatch. They molt about six times before they pupate into adult mealworms. As they molt, they leave their old skins behind in the cereal.

The beetle larva is covered in bristles.

LARDER BEETLE

Before the invention of refrigerators, larder beetles were serious pests, eating bacon, hams, dried meat and fish. The beetles cannot survive in the cold of a refrigerator.

FLIES ON MEAT

These flies are laying eggs on meat. When the larvae hatch after about 24 hours, they will grow rapidly by feeding on the nutritious meat.

Thin white eggs

FLESH EATERS

Legless fly maggots feed on meat – both dead and alive! If the female fly lays her eggs on a sheep, the maggots will eat their way into the sheep's flesh.

The maggots take just three weeks to grow from tiny grubs into adult flies.

The inside of this pea has been hollowed out by hungry seed beetles.

SEED BEETLE

The seed beetle feeds on dried peas. In parts of the world where people rely on dried peas and beans for their winter food, an infestation of seed beetles can cause food shortages.

13

WHAT A MESS!

We shed tiny pieces of our bodies every time we dress or undress, wash, shave, brush our hair, or simply move around. Wherever we go, we leave an invisible trail of hundreds of tiny particles that we only notice when they settle as layers of fluffy gray dust, or when airborne particles are caught in a ray of sunlight. Under a microscope, it is possible to see the separate hairs, fibers, skin flakes, and particles that together make up dust.

An adult sheds this much dead skin each year.

SKIN DEEP

Our skin is constantly being renewed. The older, outer layers of skin are continuously falling off in minute flakes and being replaced by layers of new skin cells underneath.

HEAT AND SWEAT

Embedded in our skin are millions of minute sweat glands. When we get hot, they squeeze out drops of salty water that evaporate and take heat away from our bodies, cooling us down.

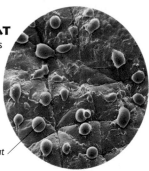

Skin flakes are soft and oily when they fall, but quickly dry and harden.

Sweat drop

BATHROOM DEBRIS

Drying yourself with a towel sends a shower of skin flakes and cotton towel fibers onto the floor, where they mix with hair, toenails, and much more.

DUST MITE

The tiny mite is 0.001 in (0.3 mm) long and feeds on flakes of dead skin. Every house is home to millions of dust mites, which live in mattresses, furnishings, and carpets. They can cause allergies.

The small blue fragments are pieces of plastic fiber from cleaning cloths.

During shaving, each hair is sliced off with a sharp blade. When highly magnified, the cut hairs look just like tree stumps.

SHAVED CHIN

All hairs grow from follicles in the skin. The hairs on a man's cheeks and chin are especially coarse. Unless a man wants to grow a beard, he has to shave every day, because the hairs soon grow back into a rough stubble.

SCRUB DOWN

Keeping clean helps us to stay healthy. Scrubbing our bodies with a soapy sponge, for example, removes grease and flakes of dead skin, and dirt that may harbor harmful bacteria. Likewise, open wounds need special care to prevent them from becoming infected. However, cleanliness does not necessarily stop us from getting skin diseases and parasites, which pass easily from person to person, especially in crowded places.

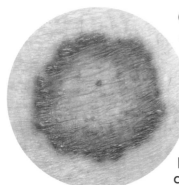

RINGWORM

Despite its name, ringworm is not a small parasitic worm but a fungal infection of the skin. It forms inflamed rings, often on the scalp. All types of ringworm are highly infectious.

SPONGES

Natural sponges are made of the skeletons of minute sea creatures that live in vast colonies, filtering and absorbing their food from the water. Synthetic sponges are made from nylon and plastic.

Synthetic sponge

Natural sponge

Water does not mix with oil but splits into drops.

Female scabies mite tunnels under the skin, leaving a long, red, itchy mark on the skin

WATER, AND OIL

Water and oil do not mix The colored water bubbles are floating in oil. Add detergent or soap and the barrier between them breaks down.

SCABIES EGGS

A female mite lays 2–3 eggs a day until she has about 25 eggs in a tunnel under the skin. The eggs hatch in 4 days. Young mites live on the skin until they are fully grown.

These eggs are lodged among flakes of skin at the entrance to a scabies mite's tunnel.

SCABIES MITE

This eight-legged mite is only just visible to the naked eye. The female scabies mite tunnels under the surface of a person's skin by biting and using a cutting edge on its front legs.

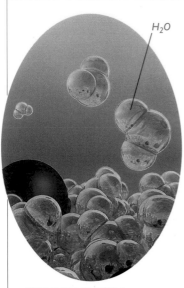

H_2O

WONDERFUL WATER

Water is a wonderful substance. Without water no living thing would be able to survive on Earth. Water is one of the very few substances that can be found in the liquid state in most parts of the world. Most substances grow denser when they change from a liquid to a solid, but liquid water becomes less dense at 39° F (4° C) before it freezes to ice, which is why ice floats on the surface of water.

EVAPORATION

A water molecule (H_2O) is made of two hydrogen atoms and one oxygen atom. Water molecules are always moving. The warmer the water, the more energy they have, and the faster they move. Evaporation occurs when surface molecules gain enough energy to escape into the surrounding air.

BOUNCING RAINDROP

When a raindrop falls in a puddle, it sets up waves that ripple outward in circles from the point of impact. The drop itself bounces up from the surface, before it falls back and becomes part of the puddle.

Highspeed photography shows a water drop recoiling from the top of a peak of water pulled from the surface of the puddle as the drop bounced.

SURFACE TENSION

The surface of water behaves as though it were covered by a stretched skin. This effect, called surface tension, is caused by the attraction of the water molecules. It is strong enough to support a razor blade.

Crystals of ice fan out over a cold windowpane.

APRIL SHOWERS

The surface of this leaf is waterproof, so each raindrop forms a round ball, held in shape by surface tension. Most leaves are designed to tip raindrops down onto the plant's roots.

ICE CRYSTALS

Liquid water forms ice as it freezes. The water molecules in ice have more space between them than the molecules in liquid water, making ice less dense.

SNOWFLAKE

Snow falling through very cold, dry air settles as distinct, individual flakes. The freezing water droplets crystallize into symmetrical hexagons with six arms. Amazingly, each single snowflake has its own unique design.

19

FIBERS AND FUR

For thousands of years, clothes were only made from natural materials. Animals provided hair, wool, and silk, while cotton, linen, and hemp were harvested from plants. Synthetic fibers, such as nylon, acrylic, and polyesters, are recent inventions. They are made from petrochemicals, which are substances derived from oil. These fibers do not rot and, unlike natural fibers, they are not attacked by insects.

NEEDLE AND THREAD

Sewing thread is made of many separate cotton fibers twisted together. When magnified, it looks very rough and weak, but the large number of entwined fibers gives the thread its strength. The surface of the thread is often smoothed before it is wound onto a cotton reel.

Individual fibers are short and thin, but twisted together they make a long thread.

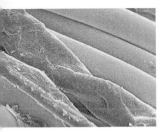

POLYESTER AND COTTON

The fabric above is a mixture of natural and synthetic fibers, and has the advantages of both materials. Cotton (gray) is absorbent and soft, while polyester (yellow) does not crease.

FUR COATS

Rabbits, like most mammals, have a soft layer of short underfur that keep them warm. This is covered by an overcoat of longer, tougher, coarser hair that protects the animal's skin and also acts as a raincoat!

Coarse outer fur

The surface of a strand of Angora wool is covered by overlapping plates.

The hooks on Velcro are permanent, easy to use, and do not wear out.

VELCRO

Minute nylon hooks on one strip of Velcro link up with the tiny nylon loops on another strip. The two strips lock tight when pressed together.

ANGORA WOOL

Angora rabbits are combed for their soft woolen undercoat.

STOP SCRATCHING!

An itchy skin is torture, but scratching only makes it worse. Bites from blood-sucking insects and other small invertebrates are a major cause of skin irritation. Some insects launch an attack only when they are hungry for blood; others trouble us because they live permanently on our skin and in our hair. An insect bite can cause an allergic response in the form of an itchy red swelling.

Nits are the egg cases of lice.

DEER TICK MOUTH
This barbed harpoon in the tick's mouth pierces a deer's thick skin. Anchored firmly by the barbs, the tick will feed on the deer's blood for several days. When the tick is full, it drops off. Ticks often transmit diseases.

Bed bugs live in the fibers of bedding material.

BED BUG
Just 0.2 in (5 mm) long, this tiny bug uses its jaws like a saw to pierce a person's skin. It then injects a stream of saliva to stop the blood from clotting. The bed bug can suck blood for up to 12 minutes before it drops off, leaving a painful bite that takes days to heal.

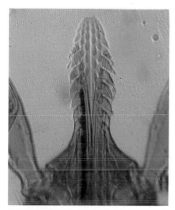

DEER TICK MOUTH
This barbed harpoon in the tick's mouth pierces a deer's thick skin. Anchored firmly by the barbs, the tick will feed on the deer's blood for several days. When the tick is full, it drops off. Ticks often transmit diseases.

STOP SCRATCHING!

An itchy skin is torture, but scratching only makes it worse. Bites from blood-sucking insects and other small invertebrates are a major cause of skin irritation. Some insects launch an attack only when they are hungry for blood; others trouble us because they live permanently on our skin and in our hair. An insect bite can cause an allergic response in the form of an itchy red swelling.

Nits are the egg cases of lice.

Bed bugs live in the fibers of bedding material.

BED BUG
Just 0.2 in (5 mm) long, this tiny bug uses its jaws like a saw to pierce a person's skin. It then injects a stream of saliva to stop the blood from clotting. The bed bug can suck blood for up to 12 minutes before it drops off, leaving a painful bite that takes days to heal.

POLYESTER AND COTTON

The fabric above is a mixture of natural and synthetic fibers, and has the advantages of both materials. Cotton (gray) is absorbent and soft, while polyester (yellow) does not crease.

The hooks on Velcro are permanent, easy to use, and do not wear out.

VELCRO

Minute nylon hooks on one strip of Velcro link up with the tiny nylon loops on another strip. The two strips lock tight when pressed together.

FUR COATS

Rabbits, like most mammals, have a soft layer of short underfur that keep them warm. This is covered by an overcoat of longer, tougher, coarser hair that protects the animal's skin and also acts as a raincoat!

Coarse outer fur

The surface of a strand of Angora wool is covered by overlapping plates.

ANGORA WOOL

Angora rabbits are combed for their soft woolen undercoat.

HEAD LOUSE EGG CASE

About 100 eggs are laid by one female head louse. She cements each egg to a strand of hair. The tiny louse nymph hatches in eight days. It punctures the egg case and inflates with air to force itself out.

RABBIT FLEA

A rabbit flea's flat body easily slips through the forest of fur. Fleas like to feed around the rabbit's ears and stomach, where the fur is less dense. Fleas are easily transferred between animals underground and can survive living on a different host.

A flea bites with a sharp blade, not teeth.

HEAD LOUSE

The widespread and irritating head louse is a flightless insect that crawls from one head to another. The louse has long claws on each foot that enable it to hold on.

A head louse needs to suck blood from its victim's scalp every three hours.

23

FABRIC FIENDS

NATURAL COMB
The dry flowerhead of a teasel plant has stiff, hooked spines. In the past, teasels were used to comb out wool to prepare it for spinning.

All clothing and blankets were once hand-made from natural fibres, and were very vulnerable to attacks by clothes moths and carpet beetles. In the wild, these insects are found in bird's nests or on the skins of dead animals. They also make their homes in people's wardrobes and munch through clothes made of natural fibers. Now that many clothes are made from synthetic fibers, life is not so easy for these damaging pests.

These firm hooks fuzz the surface of the wool without damaging the fibers.

TEASEL WORK
Today, natural and synthetic fibers are produced by automatic machinery. The hooks on teasels are still sometimes used to raise the surface pile of woolen blankets, to make them thicker and therefore warmer.

CLOTHES MOTH LARVA

Sliding through the litter of insect bodies and old feathers, this larva is at home in the bottom of a bird's nest.

Birds mistake hairy larvae for feather quills, and so do not eat them.

In this photograph the beetle has been artificially colored to make it clearer.

CLOTHES MOTH

This tiny moth lays its eggs in the folds of clothes, away from the light. When the eggs hatch, the larvae chomp holes right through the surrounding fabric.

HEAD-ON VIEW OF A CARPET BEETLE

Both the adults and larvae of this beetle chew holes in woolen material and fur. The larvae cause the most damage. Lifting a corner of an old natural-fiber carpet may reveal the hairy larvae, which are also called woolly bears.

Tough mouthparts can chew up dead insects and textiles with ease. The adults also eat pollen.

PAPER WORK

More than 5,500 years ago, the Ancient Egyptians wrote on scrolls made from the reed-like papyrus plant. The Chinese invented sheets of writing paper 2,000 years ago. All kinds of materials have been used as writing surfaces, from rags and plant fibers to animal skins. Each year we use 200–300 million tons of paper. Most of this is made from pulped wood. Increasingly, recycled paper is used as well.

GLASS PAPER

Rough pieces of wood can be rubbed smooth with glass paper. The tough paper is made from fibrous plants, such as jute and hemp. Tiny, sharp glass fragments are then glued to one side to make the rubbing surface.

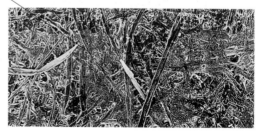

Cellulose fibers lie beneath the printed words and pictures.

NEWSPRINT

Wood is made of thousands of tiny cellulose fibers. The paper used for making newspapers, called newsprint, is made of coarse fibers from low-grade wood pulp. It is soft enough to absorb ink as it passes through high-speed printing presses.

TISSUE PAPER

Like many other types of paper, tissue paper was once the hard woody core of a tree. The wood is chipped, pulped, cooked, squeezed, beaten, dried, and finally rolled out into thin sheets.

The feathery tufts are tough fibers of cellulose in white tissue paper.

Tiny dots appear as solid colors when viewed from a distance.

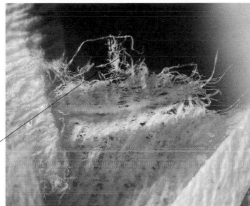

PARCHMENT

More than 2,000 years ago, people wrote on specially prepared sheets of animal skin called parchment. To make this, the skins of sheep, goats, and calves were scraped, stretched, and polished.

Chalk whitens the parchment surface.

LITHOPRINT COLOR

Color is printed onto paper in tiny dots of yellow, cyan (blue), magenta (red), and black ink. Different combinations of these four inks can print illustrations in every color imaginable.

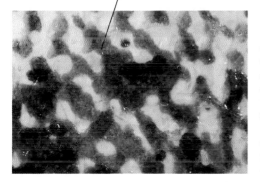

WOOD CHOMPERS

SOLDIER TERMITE
Tree-dwelling termites hollow out trunks and use the chewed wood pulp to build nursery chambers for their eggs and larvae. They will attack dead wood near the nest, including house timbers.

Some insects are specialist wood eaters. They may live beneath tree bark and feed on the tree's living tissue of sugary fibers, or produce larvae that tunnel deep into the tree trunk to feed. Other wood chompers will only attack a tree after it has died. In the gut of some insect larvae there are special microorganisms to help break down and digest the plant cellulose that wood contains. Wood-eating insects can do serious damage to furniture and house frames.

A serious attack by woodworm beetles can destroy floorboards, rafters, and furniture.

BORING!
The female woodworm beetle lays her eggs in cracks in wood. The hatchlings bore their way into the wood and feed for three years before pupating in the long tunnel they have chewed out. They emerge as adults, leaving a tiny exit hole.

THIN-SKINNED LARVA

This longhorn beetle larva feeds on dead wood. It is well hidden by the tunnel it hollows out as it eats the wood, so it has no need for camouflage or a thick skin to protect itself from predators.

Where true wasps carry a sting, the female giant woodwasp has a long egg-laying tube called an ovipositor.

All the power in this larva is in its wood-chomping jaws, which work steadily for three years or more.

GIANT WOODWASP

Formidable in appearance but quite harmless, this large insect bores deep holes in pine trees to lay eggs. Each larva grows for at least three years before chewing its way out of the tree via a long escape tunnel.

GIANT FEELERS

The male timberman beetle has antennae five times the length of its body. The beetle larvae feed on dead pine trees. If you are unlucky, you might find some living in your pine furniture!

29

NIGHT CREATURES

When the lights go out at night and you drift off to sleep, a whole host of tiny creatures emerges from cracks between floorboards, under sinks, and out of cupboards. These night creatures hide during the day to avoid predators, and only come out to feed at night.

Many creep about the kitchen, feeding on crumbs of food dropped on the floor. Others, especially spiders, lurk in corners, ready to pounce on their victims.

Venom injected from the lower jaw paralyzes the scorpion's prey.

FALSE SCORPION

These tiny predators hide away in damp crevices. They use their large "hands" and feet to feel their way around and to overpower smaller insect prey.

HOUSE CRICKET

Crickets "singing" in a warm kitchen or behind the stove were common in the days before central heating. In fact, some people kept crickets in little cages, like songbirds! Crickets do no damage and feed on scraps of food that have dropped to the floor.

The cricket makes its chirping song by rubbing its forewings together.

SILVERFISH

A silverfish is covered with overlapping silvery scales, which look like metal but are actually soft flaps of a skin-like material called cuticle.

All silverfish have poor eyesight, and emerge when it is dark to eat waste material such as food crumbs and flakes of dead skin.

HOUSE SPIDER

Spiders seem more common in autumn, when they can often be seen scampering about the floor. These are usually male house spiders searching for females to mate with.

CLOSE-UP VIEW

This silverfish is in the final larval stage. One more skin change and it will be an adult. Originally cave-dwellers, silverfish have now taken up residence in the dark places found in houses. They are often found behind books in damp rooms.

LAWN LOWLIFE

LAWN STOOLS

Autumn is the best time to look for fungi, and the lawn is a good place to start. Clusters of delicate toadstools spring up overnight, scattered through the grass or growing in rings. They shed their reproductive spores and then die within a few hours.

There's more to a neatly mown lawn than grass. Plenty of other plants and fungi flourish in the short turf. These low-growing, delicate species could not survive in longer, coarser grass. A lawn is also home to a host of insects and other invertebrates that live among the fibrous grass roots. Many feed on the nutritious roots, but some are hunters that catch and eat other creatures.

This slender toadstool has a nasty smell of ammonia.

HELVELLA TOADSTOOL

The visible part of a toadstool is its fruiting body. This contains reproductive cells that produce and release spores. We cannot see the masses of fine, underground threads, called mycelium, that collect food and water.

Cells beneath the cap of the toadstool explode and shoot out thousands of tiny spores.

SCARLET PIMPERNEL

You must look carefully to see this tiny flower in the grass. It opens in bright sunlight and closes as soon as the light fades. In the flower's center are clusters of yellow pollen.

Actual size

Yellow pollen is carried from flower to flower by insects or by the wind.

WORM WORK

A worm swallows soil, which enters its gut. Any bits of dead plants or animals are digested by the worm. The soil then passes out of the worm and may be left on the lawn as a wormcast.

EARTHWORM

Worms spend most of their time safely below ground. If the soil gets too damp, they come to the surface, where they risk being eaten by hedgehogs, birds, and shrews.

Burrowing worms improve soil quality by allowing air to enter the soil.

GLORIOUS GREENERY

All too often we take plants for granted – they are the greenery just outside the window. But a microscope reveals all sorts of extraordinary plant details: tiny veins that carry food around the plant, stinging hairs as sharp as needles, and tiny pollen grains that come in a huge variety of amazing sculptured shapes.

The spherical head snaps off when touched, leaving a sharp tip to pierce the skin.

Leaf hairs

STINGING-NETTLE HAIR
The leaves and stems of stinging nettles are covered with hollow, stinging hairs. Brushing against a nettle results in a painful injection of acid and substances called histamines.

MUGWORT
The mugwort's leaves are covered with thousands of protective hairs. They are white to reflect sunlight from the leaf's surface. The mass of hairs traps water vapor given off by the plant and prevents further evaporation.

PLANT CIRCULATION

Cells containing green chlorophyll photosynthesize to produce sugary food for the plant. Spread between them are channels called veins, which bring the cells water and take away sugar to the rest of the plant.

POLLEN BALLS

Powdery ragweed pollen is carried to another ragweed flower by the wind. Ragweed is widespread in North America, where its airborne pollen often causes hayfever.

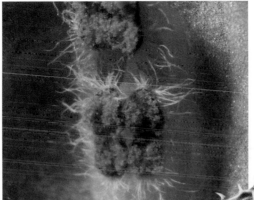

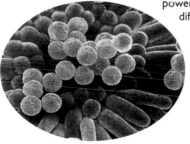

FLOWER ANTHERS

The anther is the tip of the stamen, the male part of the flower. Each anther has sacs in which pollen develops. The anthers split to release pollen grains. Some pollens are designed to be picked up by visiting insects and transferred to another plant of the same species.

HOLLYHOCK POLLEN

The details of a minute pollen grain can only be seen with a powerful microscope. Each different kind of pollen can be identified by its distinctive pattern of pores and spines, as well as by its shape.

Hollyhock pollen is round and covered with spines.

HIDE AND SEEK

Walls are full of cracks and holes that shelter all sorts of animals and plants. The small creatures that dwell in these places must endure several different and extreme environments. In summer, when the sun shines, walls become very dry and hot. When it rains, rivulets of water stream down the walls and soak into them. In winter, walls give shelter but are often freezing cold.

Moss leaf cells.

Lizard held in a hand.

MOSS
Tiny moss plants manage to survive in cracks between the bricks or stones of a wall, especially in damp spots. They absorb water and minerals from the rain.

LIVELY LITTLE LIZARD
As agile on walls as on rocky cliffs, lizards scurry about, snapping up insects and spiders. They can squeeze their flat bodies into cracks to escape from danger.

RED VELVET MITES

These mites are busy predators, even hunting down other smaller kinds of mites. They appear suddenly in great numbers, swarming over walls, rocks, and paths.

Four of the eight eyes of this spider are on the front of its head.

ROMAN SNAIL

This snail leaves a long silver trail when it wanders over a wall at night. By day, it hides in a dark place. The Ancient Romans enjoyed eating snails like this.

SPIDER EYES

Some of a spider's eight eyes are placed on its head to give it all-around vision. The two most important, large, central eyes are used for judging distances when pouncing on prey.

CENTIPEDE HUNT

At night, a wall is an excellent hunting ground for a centipede. It kills its prey by injecting it with poison from its fang-like claws.

GOOD PARTNERS

Every kind of lichen is an extraordinary partnership between two different species: a fungus and an alga. The alga contains a green pigment, chlorophyll, which absorbs energy from sunlight to make sugars. The fungus absorbs some of the sugars, and in return provides shelter for the alga. Some lichens grow to be as much as 4,500 years old. Lichens survive in the cold Arctic just as well as they do in hot deserts.

REPRODUCTION

This lichen grows like a green crust. It reproduces by soredia – tiny, powdery fragments that each contain an algal cell and fungal threads. Each soredium can produce a new lichen.

These thick, waxy lobes resemble leaves.

POLLUTION WARNING

This lobed lichen grows on rocks and tree bark, but it only grows in clean, unpolluted air. Any dissolved pollutants are absorbed by the lichen and poison it.

ANTLER LICHEN

Lichens reproduce by means of spores made by the fungal partner. In antler lichens, spores are produced in the red discs at the tips.

MUTUALLY DEPENDENT

Magnified, the cladonia lichen looks like a tree with small, smooth branches. The food-producing alga is contained within the fungus branches.

Spores are produced in these little cups on the surface of the lichen. Wind and rain blow and splash them away.

COLOR

This brightly colored lichen grows on bare rocks and is often found near the sea. It absorbs nutrients from rainwater trickling over its surface, carrying dissolved minerals. Like all lichens, it grows very slowly.

POND DWELLERS

Many pond animals start life as minute larvae, visible only as moving dots in the water, that eventually grow into much larger adults. Others, called protozoans, are tiny even when fully grown, having bodies made up of just a single cell. Only a microscope reveals their complex structure. Some of these creatures are active hunters, others float near the water's surface grabbing fragments of food, and a few stay anchored in one place.

FOOD SCRAPERS

A pond snail feeds on the slimy layer of algae that covers the underwater plant stems, leaves, and rocks in ponds and slow-moving streams. It scrapes off this nutritious layer of food using its rasping tongue, called a radula.

The radula has thousands of tiny sharp teeth arranged in rows.

SUN ANIMALCULE

This protozoan is just visible. Its fine, radiating threads trap and engulf food such as other minute protozoans.

Shrimps swim by bending and straightening their bodies as they lie sideways in the water.

FRESHWATER SHRIMP

The bottom of a pond is home to many tiny shrimps. They walk about, picking up and eating the small pieces of dead plants and animals that sink into the silt on the floor of the pond.

WATER-DROP WORLD

This magnified drop of water – no bigger than the eye of a needle – is full of female water fleas. Just imagine how many there could be in a whole pond! The swimming motion of water fleas is like underwater hopping.

The female water fleas are carrying young in their brood pouches.

Stinging cells along the tentacles help to stun prey.

HYDRA

These tiny animals are often found attached to underwater plants and pebbles. Hydra catch food by waving their stinging tentacles. This species is bright green because it contains food-producing algae.

The hydra can lengthen its body to feed.

OXYGEN MAKERS

This desmid is crescent-shaped, but its relatives have other shapes.

The smallest garden pond contains countless plants, many of them single-celled. Although tiny, their place in the pond ecosystem is vital. Not only do they keep the water supplied with oxygen, but they also form the basis of the pond food chain, because they are eaten by many pond-dwelling animals. Larger plants provide shelter for the animals that live in the pond.

DESMID

This bright-green alga consists of a single cell containing green chlorophyll. It combines the chlorophyll with energy from the sun to make food by a process called photosynthesis, releasing oxygen as it does so. The desmid moves to reach sunlit areas.

VOLVOX

A volvox is a hollow, spherical plant, with walls made from hundreds of individual cells. The cells are linked by fine threads. Each cell has two hairs that lash from side to side to roll the volvox through the water

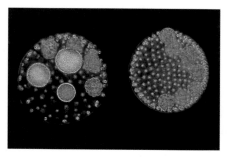

DIATOM

Diatoms are single-celled plants that photosynthesize their food. They drift in cool oceans, and some can live in fresh water. Each diatom is enclosed between two halves of a transparent silica case.

The minerals absorbed by these thin rootlets are essential for the duckweed's growth.

BLANKET WEED

The filaments, or threads, of the spirogyra alga form such a dense mass that they are known as blanket weed. Spirogyra pass the winter on the bottom of the pond as tough-walled spores.

Each cell can produce its own food. The cells join end to end to make a long filament.

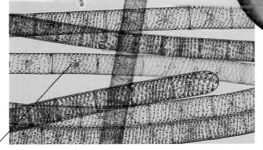

When it appears in a mass, the blue-green of the bacteria changes the color of the water.

DUCKWEED

These small individual plants cover the surface of ponds in a leafy, green sheet. Each long, delicate root absorbs nutrients from the water to supply the two or three tiny leaves to which it is attached.

BACTERIUM

Although it can photosynthesize, this tiny blue-green ball is a cyanobacterium, not an alga. It uses sunlight to make food.

SPIDERLINGS

When they hatch, spider babies cling together in a big group for a day or two. When it is time to disperse, they climb up high and spin threads of silk. The wind catches the threads, lifting the spiderlings up into the air and far away.

Young spiderlings can float in the air for hours. This is known as ballooning.

UP, UP, AND AWAY!

All young animals and plant seeds need to leave their parents and spread out, or disperse. By doing this, each one has a better chance of finding enough to eat, or enough space and light to grow. Many plants and some animals use the air to help them disperse. The tiny spores of mosses, ferns, and fungi can stay airborne even when there is no wind. Heavier seeds need parachutes or little wings to keep them in the air.

CLUBMOSS SPORES

Clubmosses are related to ferns and reproduce by spores. Before electricity was available, these spores were collected and used in the theater. When lit with a match, they explode in a bright flash.

WILLOW HERB

Each long seed pod of the willow herb opens by splitting into four parts. Each seed has its own silky parachute. The breeze catches the parachutes and carries the seeds far away from the parent plant.

The pod dries, splits and curls backwards to expose the seeds inside.

POLYPODY FERN

This fern produces its spores in tiny structures called sporangia. When the spores are ripe, the sporangia rupture and flick spores into the air.

POPLAR SEEDS

Female poplar trees produce catkins of tiny fruit. As the fruits ripen, they split open and release vast quantities of cottony fluff, in which tiny seeds are embedded.

Any remaining polypody fern spores will be blown away by the wind.

SURVIVING THE COLD

When winter arrives, life becomes difficult for many animals. Food is scarce, it is not easy to keep warm, and insects find it too cold to move or fly. Piles of decaying organic matter, such as compost heaps or dung, are warm inside. They provide a snug home and a supply of food for some tiny creatures. Some animals fall into a deep winter sleep, called hibernation, while other animals migrate to warmer climates.

Wings are well camouflaged.

PEACOCK BUTTERFLY
These insects find somewhere to hibernate in autumn, usually in a shed, outhouse, loft, or cave. They hang from a ceiling or high up on walls.

GRAY LONG-EARED BAT
There are few insects to eat in winter, so bats survive by hibernating in damp, frost-free places. They choose caves, empty buildings, or hollow trees. In the cold, a bat's heartbeat slows down. In mild weather it wakes up to drink.

HARVEST MOUSE

This tiny mouse spends winter in a nest of dry grasses. It comes out to nibble seeds or roots in warm spells. Many mice die in cold weather.

LACEWING

The green lacewing hibernates right through the winter months. Its large eyes remain open while it hibernates, but even if it sees danger approaching, it is too cold to escape.

WOODLOUSE

In cold weather, woodlice become less active than usual, but they do not hibernate. They cluster together in dark, damp places, such as under bark or beneath rocks.

ANGLE SHADES MOTH

The caterpillars of this hardy moth feed on many kinds of plant. The adult moth appears in late summer and continues to fly in midwinter if the nights are mild.

These scales must be kept moist.

These stars are the empty shells of foraminifera – single-celled protozoans that build themselves chalky shells. Star sand is made from billions of these tiny shells.

IN SAND AND SOIL

Over millions of years, the pounding of the waves on the seashore erodes rocks, pebbles, and shells into tiny particles that pile to form huge sandbanks. On the seabed there are thick layers of sediment made from the remains of dead organisms called plankton. Soil is also made by erosion, as wind and rain break down rocks. As well as rock particles, soil contains humus (decaying organic matter), bacteria, fungi, small invertebrates, and roots.

SLUDGY OOZE

Living foraminifera feed on bacteria and small plankton. When they die, their chalky shells sink to the seabed. They usually form a deep sediment called foraminiferous ooze.

Spiral foraminifera

GROUND ROOTS

Plants grow best in moist, airy, fertile soil. Plant roots divide into fine rootlets that spread out through the soil to absorb moisture and nutrients.

Water is absorbed through cottony hairs right at the tip of each rootlet.

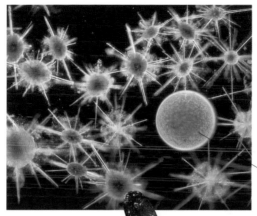

RADIOLARIA

Tiny protozoans called radiolaria drift in the upper layers of the oceans. Their round, spiky skeletons are made from silica. When they die, their skeletons fall to the seabed and are eventually ground down to form sand.

An invader in the radiolaria flotilla

WIREWORM

This click beetle larva, called a wireworm, lives underground only while it is a larva. It is a garden pest, because it eats plant roots.

ANT LIFE

Ants live in underground nests. They live in the upper parts of the nest in summer, but retreat to lower levels in winter to escape the frost. Some ants kill other creatures and drag them down into their nests to eat them.

Smooth and shiny, wireworms slip easily through the soil.

BESIDE THE SEA

When paddling or swimming in the sea, you are sharing the water with millions of larval sea animals that are invisible to the naked eye. Many sea creatures – from tiny invertebrates to large fish – produce hundreds, thousands, or even millions of eggs. They need to do this, because so many of their tiny offspring are eaten by larger animals and never reach maturity. They are one of the first stages in the ocean food chain.

FISH EGGS
Some of these round fish eggs are hatching. Many fish produce eggs that float in the warmer water near the surface of the ocean. Each egg contains a tiny yolk and droplets of oil to feed the developing embryo.

A wood-boring grub leaving timber exposed to salt water.

DRIFTWOOD
Wood from trees, wrecks, and storm damage may be washed into the sea. It is eventually cast onto the shore as driftwood. On land, dead wood is slowly chewed by wood-boring insects, but in the sea teredo worm molluscs bore deep holes into submerged timber.

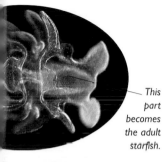

LARVAL STARFISH
A young starfish goes through a number of stages as it grows. Sometimes it swims freely, and sometimes it is attached to the ocean floor by a stalk.

This part becomes the adult starfish.

BIG-EYED LARVA
The transparent larva of the matid shrimp has huge, goggle eyes that are quick to detect the slightest movement of any prey. It is a greedy hunter and killer.

Front legs seize prey.

This lava looks quite unlike its spiky parent.

SENIOR SEA CUCUMBER
Sea cucumbers burrow into mud on the ocean floor. When disturbed, some shoot out sticky tubules to entangle their attackers. Others defend themselves by throwing out their internal organs. New organs grow in their place.

JUNIOR SEA CUCUMBER
A sea cucumber larva is called an auricularia because of its ear-like flaps.

RECYCLING

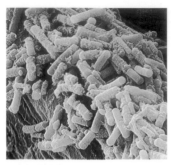

BACTERIA
These rod-shaped bacteria are found in the straw and dung of farm animals. They break down plant material in the dung and absorb it as food. They reproduce rapidly by dividing two or three times every hour.

Nature has its own recycling service in the form of scavenging creatures that feed on dead plants, animals, and animal dung. Left uneaten, these remains would cover the ground and take years to rot before they could become a useful part of the soil. Nature's recyclers are everywhere, but most of them are found in dung, compost, and animal debris. Some are specialists that eat only one kind of rubbish, but others will feast on whatever organic remains they can find.

Dung ball

ROLL ON
The male beetle collects dung, rolls it into a ball, and buries it. The female beetle lays her eggs in the dung ball. The beetle grubs eat the dung when they hatch.

EARWIG

An earwig will eat any organic remains it finds, whether they are animal or vegetable. Earwigs are widespread in gardens, where they can find food easily.

Earwigs do have wings, but they seldom fly.

LEOPARD SLUG

A fully-grown leopard slug may be as long as 8 in (20 cm). It prefers to eat soft, rotting plant material, rather than chew on tougher tissues.

WORM RECYCLERS

Brandling worms break down organic material, such as plant litter, by eating it. When they expel it from their bodies, it becomes part of the soil. The nutrients in this recycled waste help to make the soil more fertile.

Masses of worms can survive on concentrated organic matter.

GIANT BLACK MILLIPEDE

Millipedes are vegetarians. This tropical species is a very efficient recycler. It spends its life chewing up dead leaves, which it passes out of its body as droppings that enrich the forest soil.

Slugs pick up the smell of food using their tentacles.

53

INDEX

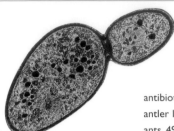

Yeast cells

Sugar beet crystals

D

desmid, 42
diatoms, 43
diseases, 4, 16, 22
driftwood, 50
duckweed, 43
dung, 46, 52
dung beetle, 52
dust, 14, 15

E

earthworms, 33
earwigs, 53
ecosystems, ponds, 42
eggs:
  clothes moths, 25
  flies, 13
  head lice, 23
  scabies, 17
  sea animals, 50-1
erosion, 48

evaporation, 18
eyesight, 4

F

false scorpion, 30
ferns, 44, 45
fibers, 20, 21, 24
fish, 50
fleas, 23
flies, 13
flowers, 33
food, 6-7
  pests, 12-13
  rotting, 10-11

food chain, 50
food poisoning, 11
foraminifera, 48
fruiting bodies,
fungi, 33
fungi:
  in food, 8, 9
  lichen, 38-9
  ringworm, 16
  rotting food, 10-11
  spores, 11, 33, 44
  toadstools, 32-3
fur, 21, 23

G, H

grain weevils, 12
grass, 32-3
gray long-eared bat, 46

hair, 5, 15
  head lice, 22, 23
  shaving, 15
hairs, on plants, 34
harvest mice, 47
head lice, 23
helvella toadstool, 33
hemp, 20, 26
hibernation, 46-7
hollyhock, 35
house dust mites, 15
human debris, 14-15
humus, 40
hydra, 41

I, J, K

ice, 18, 19
insects:
  blood-sucking, 22-3
  in clothes, 20, 24-5
  in food, 12-13
  in lawns, 32
  in winter, 46-7
  wood-eating, 28-9, 50
itching, 22-3

jute, 26

L

lacewing, 47
larder beetle, 13
larvae:
  carpet beetles, 25
  clothes moths, 25
  in food, 12, 13
  pond life, 40
  sea animals, 50-1

wireworms, 49
wood-eating insects,
  28, 29
lawns, 32-3
leaves, 19, 34
Legionnaire's disease, 4
leopard slugs, 53
lice, 23
lichen, 38-9

*Snow
flake*

linen, 20
lizards, 36
longhorn timber
  beetles, 29

M

maggots, 13
mantid shrimp, 51
mealworms, 12
meat, 6, 13
mice, 47
microscopes, 4
millipedes, 53

mites, 5, 15, 17, 37
molecules, water, 18-19
moss, 36, 44
moths, 24, 25, 47
molds, 8-9, 10-11
mugwort, 34
mycelium, 33

N, O

natural fibers, 20, 21
needles, 20
nests:
  ants, 49
  birds, 24, 25
newsprint, 26
nits, 23
nuts, 11
nylon, 20

oil, 20
oranges, 10
oxygen, 18, 42

P

paper, 26-7
papyrus, 26
parachutes, seeds, 44,
  45
parasites, 16
parchment, 27

Stubble on a chin